JN418484

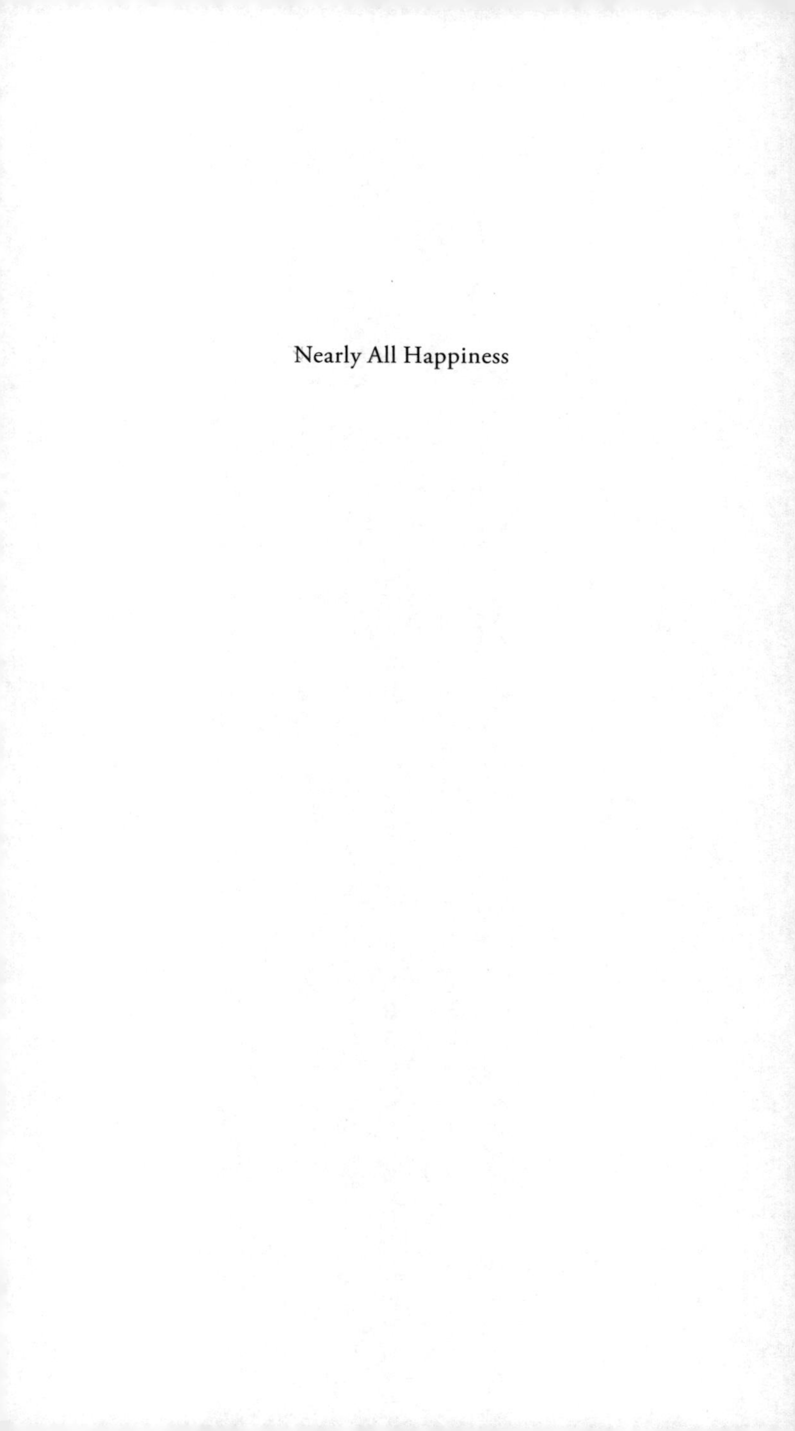

Nearly All Happiness

Nearly All Happiness

A collection of new poems by Lee Soyoun
Translated by Sunnie Chae

Contents

NEARLY ALL HAPPINESS

The Conflict of Interpretations

I hope clever minds die unknowing
who my father is,
be it Lee, Lee, or Lee.

I somehow loved only Lees,
my mother tells me.

Though words are shed, people die in those shells,
hence the eternal shedding.

I grow ashamed of my parts without pairs,
the sole heart, tongue,
stomach, and navel.

No wonder the buttocks are split.

Tomorrow will I sin better than today.

Navel-gazing snaps your neck.
Curious to see, you open a cellar
that locks you in, they say.

Falling away leaves that dimpled mark.

When radishes I choose are hollow,
she says they resemble me.
I take after her, the one who bore me.

“Wait till you have a daughter like you.”

While a blemish begets a blemish,
Lee is no father figure or master.
Lee is a name against the idol,
transcending him, the father.

I sense something missing at home.
I know not what.

Life of the Other

Quiet flames on a gas stove, hushed music,
silence parading past groveling words.

The first snowfall reaches a hand's width
as I boil tea water in the morning at 9 a.m.

Sunlight seeps from without to within
as we keep ourselves down.

Believing what is said and not said too,
between knees do I beg forgiveness.

The gas was inspected,
but do I smell a leak?
My feet fall as softly as snow

for I fear you might kill me.

Come here, child.
A meek one raised to bear out belief.

The tea seems stained with blood.
I see tea dust sinking,
drowning like eyelashes.
To live, I must leave.

Spittle turns unclean outside the mouth.
My shadow drags behind outdoors.

Monstrously Feminist Man

A man likes to wash, clean, and cook.
Once you meet and marry this man,
he will be ironing blouses in a sunny room,
claiming credit for it all, even for your childbirth.

I will be face down in bed till 10 a.m.,
sleep staying with me as my husband leaves for work.
Fixing breakfast, commuting with our child in tow,
his feminist ritual for an ordinary wife.

At times, I echo my mother-in-law.
Oh Lord . . .

I vacuum promises easily dropped.
Be mindful, Son. No more messy crumbs.
Birthed by C-section. Little did I know.
Oh Lord . . .

I reproach myself as always.
Propped on a toilet, recalling the winding hours of morning,
feeling like an elephant.

The elephant appreciated only at the zoo
has a nose for hands, hands for feet.
Men have nipples, those ornamental teats.
It makes me wonder about purpose and use.

A man with morning sickness
grows a pregnant belly like mine.
As he breathes Lamaze-style next to me,
I take my placenta out for him,
the pure, circumcised man I love
enough to transplant my organs.
I pen this age-old prophecy
born out of days and nights of prayer.

Oh Lord . . .

I yield my every right to you. Take this holy child.
That this labor of mine may now be yours,
I give you my spasms of pain,
uterine muscles, contractions, all that I am.

No credit to me, a leeching wife.
I stand on the Metro by the priority seats,
on my feet till delivery.

Supper is a messy dish of taco rice.
Shredded lettuce falls with each bite.

Partial Solar Eclipse

The birthday winds down
and nearly all happiness wanes,
about to grow false.
A face pushed into frosting
spares a single slice of truth
once the candles are out.
Reluctant to finish
that one piece intact,
friends say goodbye,
leaving leftovers behind.
I clear away half-empty cups, forlorn.
My soul is soothed after the party.

A photo of us with the cake
shows how it was whole.

I stop hearing from a friend
who used to share photos of red-crowned cranes.
There are no more cranes to be seen.
Are they alive?
Why are we prone to sadness,
detaching from rare things
that elude us by misfortune?
The sun is eclipsed
during my sedated endoscopy.
I gaze skyward in my sleep.
Erasures go unnoticed unless you know.
When an eclipse does not darken,
when an attachment leads nowhere,
knowing is all we can do.

Someone taps me on the shoulder,
waving and fading into summer.

Boundaries

An A-bomb drops unbeknownst to me.
Do I see beauty in its midst?
I am flung into a bathroom corner by that thunderous roar,
abuse, blast, exposé, barrage, death, tempest, and storm.

Landing hard on the floor,
I melt down in the heat,
loving you in your rage.
You thrust me aside,
but in love I remain.

Let us not think of beauty.

Do not see the forest for trees,[*]

do not see the ruin for rubble.

Though my face has collapsed,

I am still alive.[**]

I drive a nail in the wall,

step gingerly off a chair.

Like sand treading the beach

with crumbling lips,

* Francis Ponge, "Le cycle des saisons" in *Le parti pris des choses* (1942; Paris: Gallimard, 2009).

** Fukuda Sumako, *Ware nao ikite ari* (1967; Tokyo: Chikuma Shobo, 1982).

I hate nothing.

Yesterday's shriveling skin
teaches me the pain of cloth.

Will the breeze lift my pain and leave a pattern?
I feel my soles tingle.

I ask limbs as frail as butterfly legs,
why are you still beautiful?
To leave beauty behind,
passing through alive.

Hackberry Tree

A child swings from a 600-year-old hackberry tree.

Left behind are things that grow
like snakeskin and leaves.

If only you and I could survive six centuries.

The hackberry tree never had lasting company.

In loving do we age.

Only trees stay flourishing.
Aging evermore, fueling fondness.

The heart is a child's hackberry in a sling.

Some trees fall or go ablaze.
Others reach hoary age
like grande dames
standing stately and tall.

You are laid up with an ache.
Far off, I see the hackberry tree.
Longer, longer must I go.

Ping, rushing to comfort,
doomed to love.

Oldest Possession

Rummaging through a drawer,
I come across cucumber seeds.

Mom saw cucumber in her baby dream.
But why do I find these?

I do not grow a garden
although I believe in seeds.

They seem alien to me.
Did my pen pal send them
before losing touch?
I find no mention in old letters.

My thoughts return to Mom.

Dad hit her when she chided Gran
for picking cucumber too soon.
Villagers swarmed the house,
forced soap water down her throat.
I looked away from her vomit.

Seeds used to sprout awake,
open their fists,
and climb roofward in spring.

She kept pesticide for those vines.
I was still too young.

These seeds could grow
into long-faced cucumber.

I would rather keep them

as my oldest possession,

carefully labeled *cucumber seeds.*

Bobby Pin

I envy the sunset shining through glass.
I rarely gain easy entry.

I set off metal detectors in buildings.
Feeling heavily armed,
I open doors to unknown worlds
where I find eyes staring me down.

I cannot pass beyond myself or explain.

Alarms go off.
I tell myself I am innocent.
I merely wrote poems called "Steel."

Blood rushing, skin heating,

I nearly take a leak as the guard draws near.

A friend of mine has a metal detector.
That night, I dream of being hit by a meteorite.
It lodges in me. My knees creak.

Steel dissolves into red, rusty puddles.

Imagination of the Earth

The sprawling earth lies looking peaceful.
This tree withers as that tree digs deep.
A terrible drought begins.
I peer into the imagination of the Earth.*

Trees tear at me, reaching for water.
They say it runs through my name.
My liver and bowels crumble.
I see writhing roots lodged in me.

I push away leaves that cut my fingers.
With my toes, I briefly shake the ground.

* Jongcheol Kim, *Imagination of the Earth* (Seoul: Green Review Publishing, 2019).

My head is a woodland tombstone
or a female Buddha in banyan roots.

Which will survive, Mother Earth or trees?
I lie feeling wooden to the core.
Trees become *The Book of Disquiet*, transporting me.*
Roots feel creatures in the earth,
moles, worms, ants, burrowing by necessity.

Birds fly toward leaves and canopies.
I take note of how they sing and perch.
Draping summer over Mother Earth

* Fernando Pessoa, *The Book of Disquiet*, trans. Richard Zenith (1982; New York: Penguin Books, 2002).

with small openings for light, wider ones for rain.

Imagination of the Earth on a summer's day.

Nesting in Stone

I plan to hold a molten city in me.
Slowly will I cool down.
In time, I will harden like granite,
grained with age-old humanity.

A small disaster will do the trick,
but disasters are rarely small.
Just as a brandished knife
fatally stabs the flesh,
birds and boughs dissolve.
None can nest in stone.

Legions of trees perish into paper.
Thoughts falter like newborn fawns.

Customs fade, revealing an end.

I salvage a blue-sky title,
pulled from one last pocket of life.
As a faithful scribe, I must shun all faith.

The dying Earth spins.
Rain falls, undeterred.

I return home.

I reflect on why we shelter from the rain.
Then I sing, embracing death.
Improvised melodies mingle
with the laughter of friends.

And it all turns to stone.

Bed Sores

Was it lying on a vine?
A lizard drops its tail to escape.
Tubers that healed underground
emerge to see the light of day.

So many sweet potatoes
grown from vine cuttings.

The hollows they leave are filled with dirt.
Mom lays them out, rolling them dry.

The sun shines on that still life,
a neatly lined arrangement.

The nursing home garden
reminds me of Gran in her bed.
Mom turns her this way and that,
warning me of skin being pressed.
I imagine lips.

Fresh stems drop roots like IV drips,
strong enough to lift the ground.

Shipped home, sweet potatoes last too long,
growing moldy in their box.

"A short life is a blessing—"
The lizard breaks off as it flees.

Being Sea-Born

Paradise bears the mien of Jukdo Market
where a good man's knife slices silvery gills.
Blood spills, the bowed horizon lies flat.
I held my first knife at seventeen.
My arms grew lopsided since then.

Pohang Harbor rarely sees snow.
Snow bodes well for gilled fellows.

This is no dream,
only a city growing pale,
muttering that by falling you live,
falling without as within.

The tongue catches snowflakes

tasting of rockfish.

If all that hails from sea is sea-born,
so too is snow.

Then what about bones,
death in the body?

I have much to say
to those surviving without dying.
Tales of blood for the undying dead
lasting half a century outside life.
Speaking like the snowfall
that snow is sea-born
from whence I pick bones.

Time punctures being.

None in the tank believe me.

Clothespins

They tend to be damp,
our ruminated thoughts.

Futile waste in a bin.
Am I reminded of a tub?

I see in this town
too many basins filled.

Therein breath lingers.
Death tarrying long.

Pulled like washing from a womb,
I live by turning pages.
Holding dear reminders close,

tiny socks pegged on a clothesline.
I wonder what cannot be tossed.

I reach into the bin.
Pick up what is yours.

A few I turn inside out to dry.

Shaking the wrinkles out of jealousy,
turning the sleeves of a dragging night,
hanging night dry, waiting for the morning bus.

Fear not.
Banghak-dong's poet is bound to live long.

Dead Tree

They deliver blows
but never return.

I am determined to die standing.

The dying are yet alive.

Crabs heaped on a market stall
wave their claws when struck.
You strike at the dying
to see that they live.

I cheat life
as crustaceans do.

Waving arms in the wind,
gazing down.

Who pounds on my chest?

"Believe not what others say."
I wish to believe that saying.

Cheating drives evolution.*

Life persists
when no one else protects it.

* Steven Pinker, *The Blank Slate: The Modern Denial of Human Nature* (New York: Viking Press, 2002).

Powerful ones dwell without.

I grow hollow within.

Our death evolves,

returning under guise.

Noon wanes over us.

How we love what saps our blood.

Inhaling Verdure

We resolve to stay home,
but homes lead outdoors.
Mine leads me out itself.

It seeks out a corpse tree,*
asking how it stays still.
Why do its leaves look down?
Why do ants shy away?

Such is the joy of company,
like an umbrella when it pours.
Rain soaks my trouser hems.

* The East Asian orixa colloquially known as *songjang namu* or "corpse tree."

I see a flooded world above.

How good to be a remedy.
Brushing hands as we walk,
sharing the same thoughts,
breathless without a word.
Stepping off a train, we see a dead doe.
"Should we get her off the road?"
The warm body saddens.
I once tried to save you from me.

They say love stretched far
will stop like the rain.
"Do you hear raindrops?"

Catching our breath,
we gaze down on houses.
A roof, roof, and roofless green.
Inhaling verdure, we return each to our homes.

A Classicist Squinting

I do as told,
following guidelines to a tee.

I remove pilling from a pocket.

Does moss eat into stone?
Or does stone feed on moss?

I teach at a college,
saying class postponements will be brief.
An optimistic preamble to calamity.

I pay taxes on time,
record lectures on Roubaud,
visit trees and squint skyward.

I know little of death though Dad has passed.
Mom stays longer on the phone with me.
I walk my child to school thinking of mortality.
The booster shot, a dose of hope.

Time to grind coffee at 9 a.m.
Shoes, books, hats, and bags
all drip with blood this year.

My child rolling snowballs outdoors
unluckily steps on dog mess.
I scrape it off her boot soles.

They say life is in the living.

I trudge on with my thoughts,
observing anniversaries on the way.
What day is it today?

May a blank page quiet a stubborn mind.

At the Breakfast Table

Gaia's nausea was gone.
So was last night's vomit,
cleaned up without a trace.
How did she recuperate?
It was hard to believe.

A woman had slept by her husband.
Why was she bothering a man and wife?
Gaia had tossed and turned to push her away.

She asked her husband in the morning,
eating the rice and soup he cooked.

Who was she last night?
Who do you mean?

I dreamt of a woman in our bed.

Then tell me, who was he?
Who do you mean?
I dreamt of a wife-snatching man.

Her husband made coffee.
Gaia mused about her suitor.

He had dropped a book.
She found one under the table
titled *Love What You Pick Up*.

Gaia could not speak of that man.
She could not hear of that woman.

Fist

Neighborhood doctors jokingly say,
were this a clinical trial,
the vaccine would be a flop.
Today I get my booster shot.

Fifteen minutes,
and a rash climbs up my arm.
"Look . . ."
"Let's get you a jab in the buttocks."
Leaning and waiting exposed,
I imagine the world's bottom
and one big shot to rid us of hate.

From a taxi on a long road,
I see protesters advancing,

holding defeatism at bay,
pumping fists, yelling slogans.
Green light, and their signs go ablur.

Neither for nor against,
I suffer.
Being used to suffering,
I suffer.
From headache,
from fever,
from doorbells too.
Unknown suffering leaves a package.
Wind suffers from branches,
snow from its own purity.

Even the snowman is masked,
made in our image.

I lie in bed wondering if it has a mouth.

In the haze of a dream, I suffer.
I am surrounded by mice,
chased by a beastly god.

That night of suffering behind me,
I visit the doctor for an IV drip.
The nurse getting me ready
asks me to make a fist.

White Radish

I find a radish
hence slice a radish.

A pale, white root.

Gripped by fate,
it grew underground
and lost its hue.

He asks for water.
Fearing it might kill him,
I reluctantly refuse.

Out of surgery for lung cancer,
he would risk all for a sip.

I bike along Hyeongsan River
toward the seaside factories.
Heavy rain like shredded radish
falls amid their chimneys.

Hoping for a flavor swelling up umbrella-like,
I clear my mind and slice a radish.

I find a radish in the fridge,
hence I slice a radish.

I Know Not of USS *Arizona*

USS *Arizona* rests in water
after all that has passed.
Eroding, still sinking.
I hear wafting waves.

I dream of parting with water.

He used to pour water away,
wary of attachment.

It struck me as a question mark.
Can past lovers ever be friends?
American-style partners, perhaps.
Not that I would know.

A tree has fallen on the beach.
Sunday morning topples over beds.

Delicate feelings corrode.
I wish mine to be like bent nails,
broken shards of chinaware,
useless and easily disposed.

Love roams the beach.
I speak to a stranger.

Oil seeps steadily out.

A man who never joked since then

discusses deep-seated history.

USS *Arizona* ripples across his lips.

I wonder how deep it lies.

Is it history that lies therein?

I wait for bodies to rise.

The beach crowds.

Unawaited, war begins.

POET'S NOTE

The Body's Stories

"Mom, keep your mask on at home, alright? We don't want Dad getting infected too." Upon being released from COVID-19 home isolation, I learned that my mom tested positive. She kept worrying about me instead of herself. She fussed, "Why is your body so frail? Are you feeling better now?"

Three vaccine shots had already riddled my body with side effects. By the end of a week-long isolation, my nipples began leaking fluid. I was told the COVID treatment's digestive meds were to blame. Life had long since annexed my body for its dirty work. Cockroach and rye allergies, hemorrhoids caused by chronic constipation, a bout of thyroid cancer, an induced abortion, and a childbirth—such were the travails of my body. Lousy experiences for sure, but nothing too serious. With this body, I managed to love again and again. Tugging at the hand of a significant other to pop in and out of roadside shops and stroll up the Namsan Mountain Trail. With so much to love in the world, no sadness was too heavy to cast aside. Troubling events were soon forgotten. I was a gifted purger of memory. Like dried flowers resuscitated in a watered vase, I revived my own heart. Even shaking off traumas. And yesterday, I read Annie Ernaux's *Happening*. The protagonist Anne initially believes that male and female bodies are no different in their experience of love and passion. I once tried to believe the same. I used to be free in sexual expression. Lacking gender awareness, I never contemplated the gendered underpinnings of discriminatory sayings and doings. I had a tendency to avoid all thought regarding the possibility that I, as a woman, might be subject to gender discrimination. My fervent resistance to injustice had stemmed only from my standpoint as an individual human being.

My parents, who desperately hoped for a son, ended up with two daughters. Circumstances made them speak like new-born feminists. Times had changed, they said. No one deserved to face unjust discrimination since men and women were equal. I took them at their word, believing we lived in a new era. Hence the world I knew was a beautiful place. I dreamed of attending KNPU, the Korean National Police University. To make myself fit, I began learning hapkido as a sixth-grader, keeping it up until my sophomore year in senior high. After practice, I used to play Johnny-on-a-Pony with the boys.[*] I would bend over to put my head under their crotches, unashamed. No one thought to make anything of it. I only cared about toppling them, landing on their backs as hard as possible when it was my turn to leap. Alas, I lacked the brains to enter KNPU.

I never experienced any gender discrimination of note while living under my parents' roof. Once I moved away for university, I realized the world was stranger than I thought it was. But being rather carefree, I managed just fine. That is, until I felt it for myself. Female unfreedom, the kind of unfreedom Mrs. Rawlings faces in Doris Lessing's "To Room Nineteen."

Every so often at the bus station, I became the target of lewd sexual advances. I told my boyfriend only to hear in reply, "It's because you wore a

* The Korean version of the game is known as *maltagi* (horse riding) or *malttukbakgi* (piling).

skirt." University parties with alcohol also came with pervs. I grew frightened of a strange man who began leaving items at my door every day. I eventually relocated to escape. It was terrifying to have a stalker, but my boyfriend blamed me, not him, finding fault with my behavior. It made me want to die. After a series of these incidents, I saw just how oblivious I had been. I began feeling suffocated, even by the solicitude shown to me as a woman. With a few exceptions, most of this solicitude came across as ostentation. "Look at what I'm doing for you now," they seemed to say in a ritual display. Completed with that smug look of a superior stooping to share a handicap. Whatever freedom I gained as a result was not true freedom. I came to see that patronizing display for what it was: a dreadful way of rendering my freedom an aberration.

"Why are you so sensitive?" So were women told when they raised the issue of gender discrimination. But no woman had grown sensitive without cause. Our society, state, and laws had to be questioned more than our women. Crimes against the female body were horrendous; the discrimination and prejudice that followed, even more so. But I did not want to collapse. Writing poetry required that I constantly reaffirm my womanhood. Hence I resisted all things that fueled negative emotions about my body. Though my voice was feeble, I thought, *Let us read more works by women. Our love will strengthen them, and that will bring about change. We will acknowledge them.*

Five years ago, I penned an essay while finding my place amid the many layers of feminism. I wrote, "Gender exists within the problem of power. And power is not obtained easily by haphazard means. I wish for us women to approach the establishment of gender power in a more sophisticated manner. Antagonistic attacks will achieve nothing. Setting up new dynamics and stirring controversy are two different matters. The former lays the foundation for persuasion whereas the latter only wastes your breath.

"There exists a plethora of feminist works. Works by female poets as well as those female novelists shunned by certain male readers for not suiting their taste. I wish for us to read, share, and mention these works together. Each writer struggles to endure their own world, albeit in different ways. No writer would create a work that failed to persude them. It is too late to expect feminist works from Kim Su-young or Baudelaire. I no longer wish to be disillusioned by writers long dead. The task falls on us. We must pursue promising ways of enhancing gender power. That is why some believe that cooperation for the sake of female gender power will, in the long run, benefit male gender power as well."

Many writers have written since then. I have written myself. In the past, we wrote and read among ourselves, but now they, too, read what we write. Their writing differs from the past. Gone is the anger. Only a pure, boundless curiosity about the world remains. Also, the story of feelings unknowingly endured. In such sentences, I see hope. I learn to accept, standing firm.

POET'S ESSAY

An Illness that Renders All the World into Poetry

What is this?

A poem.

What is that? A poem.

I caught an illness that rendered all the world into poetry.

I saw it coming.

I met and married a poet. I then gave birth to our child. I have been with my husband for over a decade. By now, it is time we grow weary, but I never weary of him. Perhaps because he lives in this world that preoccupies me. Holding hands, we walk along Banghak Stream. Wherever he points, I find a poem. On some days, taking the form of ducks; on others, taking after white-naped cranes.

Black koi swirl the clear water like brush strokes, and therein lies another poem. A poem rippling. Scattering. Startling tiny minnows. Fleeing from grey herons.

People walking their dogs have poems too. Dogs speak with their noses, those glossy vessels for canine words. Dogs never tread toward bad smells. They seek out freshness. Fragrant places. Humans are not the ones dragging their dogs out for a walk; dogs are the ones dragging their humans out instead. Dogs prefer side trails. The untrodden paths where you glimpse grassy thoughts. Humans stay on cement pavement; dogs urge toward dirt roads. Wanting us to see our footsteps and reflect on our lives. Perhaps as a prescription for passing through this pandemic time.

My husband seems to point to a poem, not a dog. Whenever we share what we see, we often say, "It's a poem!" It stirs things into becoming poetry. I find poems in conversation, relishing in this life of discovery.

Even in the chance words of a friend, I encounter a poem. "An absolute poem!" I think about asking if I could use it, but then I think again. That friend is the poet Kim Eunji, who wrote "*Goguma* and *Gomawo* Share Two Syllables." Knowing that even a two-syllable overlap inspires her to celebrate in verse, I find myself wary of asking for her words whether she plans on using them or not. Like soap bubbles, a poem rises and vanishes within me. That is more than enough. Not every poem is completed, but their moments matter. Poetry is not a goal but a drive that sustains me as a poet. My life depends on its continuity.

Last winter, I saw a snowman with a sign on its chest reading, "I'll head back once the weather clears." Whoever made that snowman must have peered into their own soul. It made me think of a person who had a place whereto return. I saw a poem in that snowman. The first poem I remember writing came from a snowman too. It was a diary entry.

It happened when I was eight years old. All our neighbors made snowmen in their backyards. I made one too. My younger sibling and I did as Mom told. Blindly following her orders, we rolled balls of snow and found pebbles. An outgrown church kindergarten hat topped off the snowman. It look disgruntled. Building the snowman with Mom made me wonder whose it was. I had wanted to make my own snowman, but I built one that Mom wanted instead. I could not shake the belief that, though built together, the snowman was hers. Built to her plan. I could hardly see my soul in it.

"Mom, whose snowman is this?" I asked. "Yours, Soyoun." I was surprised. Was it fair to call it mine? My young and innocent sibling burst into tears. So for a while, we called it my sibling's. But I still believed it was Mom's. I wrote about it in my diary that day. That gave me my own snowman. We built a snowman together, each remembered different ones, and mine became a poem. A poem is not easily made yours, even when offered by others, but once fully yours, it belongs to no other. That to me is poetry. Seeing poems pervading all things, I can never weary of the world.

COMMENTARY

Loving Capability

Kim Eunji (Poet)

I know the one and only way to anger Lee Soyoun. Calling plants and animals by the wrong names. “I smell perilla leaves,” I said, pausing in Gongneung-dong’s Railroad Park. “Are those perilla leaves?” “What?” came the indignant response. Soyoun declared that they were most definitely not perilla leaves, that it was an egregious error to mistake them for such, and pulled a sad face as if her feelings were hurt.

Using a smartphone app, we learned that the plant was a sunroot nicknamed *ttungttanji* or “hooey.” “No more hooey about it being perilla.” Once we shared a chuckle, Soyoun grew serious again. “Perilla leaves are much rounder and have fuzzy hair.”

As a country girl who grew up with nature as her playground, Soyoun made a point of taking interest in such finer distinctions and remembering them. She gazed awhile at the sunroot as if determined not to forget its name. Unless plants or animals are misnamed, Soyoun finds no cause to be angry. With time being short, she spends her life loving instead.

I love Soyoun. I can write this sappy sentence because I feel her love. Soyoun loves her family, loves her friends, loves her readers, loves this Earth, loves the sunroot, and loves poems. Everyone loves. But when Soyoun loves, she does her utmost to shower affection, letting others feel it. Endlessly replenished, her love seems to grow the more it is shared. It fascinates me. What if she shares more affection than she can handle? What if others take it for granted, demanding even more as if it were their due? Upon observation, I learn that those showered by affection cherish her in return, looking out for her.

I read her poems hoping to find the secret behind this loving capability. Her first poetry collection is titled *I Need a Girl Who Will Die Slowly*. The eponymous girl lives in a manner in keeping with her true self. The title reveals a painful awareness that, within a society tightly interlaced with conventions unjustly oppressive toward women, she must discard her self-as-girl in order to survive. The title also conveys the poet's ingenious decision to have that girl "die slowly," delaying the inevitable for as long as possible.

The collection's first poem "Steel" ends with the sentence, "It no longer seemed strange to find steel wire by the sea." The speaker is a six-year-old girl who, upon closing her eyes to hear the sea, gets her cheek torn by a barbed wire fence. She wonders why the fence goes unremoved, but it stays in place until she no longer finds it strange.

Without anyone to clear such things away, the world remains a dangerous place where "a cellar . . . locks you in" in "The Conflict of Interpretations," "[t]he heart is a child's hackberry in a sling" in "Hackberry Tree," and "leaves . . . cut my fingers" in "Imagination of the Earth," wounding and endangering the innocent. The speaker of "Inhaling Verdure" muses:

How good to be a remedy.
Brushing hands as we walk,
sharing the same thoughts,
breathless without a word.
Stepping off a train, we see a dead doe.
"Should we get her off the road?"
The warm body saddens.
I once tried to save you from me.

They say love stretched afar
will stop like the rain.
"Do you hear raindrops?"

"We" cannot walk past a dead doe, roadkill in all likelihood. Letting sadness seep in while clearing away that doe in the rain, the speaker recognizes the action as an attempt to "save you from me." Such is love, a deep-reaching, life-altering process as well as a palpable, sensory experience that can "stop like the rain."

In "Partial Solar Eclipse," the poet "clear[s] away half-empty cups, forlorn." Having this image in mind changes the tone of other poems as I reread them. In "Clothespins," the poet speaks:

Holding dear reminders close,
tiny socks pegged on a clothesline.
I wonder what cannot be tossed.

I reach into the bin.

Pick up what is yours.

A few I turn inside out to dry.

The common saying "pick up after yourself" no longer sounds cold. To love is to pick up what is yours. Could it begin from cleaning up the world and thus clearing the way for true happiness and delight? Perhaps doing so makes it possible to transcend irony and impossibility, whether it be "[b]elieving what is said and not said too" in "Life of the Other," "[a]n optimistic preamble to calamity" in "A Classicist Squinting," or the statement that "Lee is a name against the idol" in "The Conflict of Interpretations."

I wonder if I might be doing Soyoun a disservice by describing her as some sort of guardian spirit of plants and animals when in reality she is merely living as her true self. Nevertheless, having long since followed her writing career from nearby, I must say that love is the common theme and structure running through her work.

I ring her up to double-check.

"Do you remember the name of that plant I mistook for a perilla?"

"Sunroot?"

Smiling, I end our call.

WHAT THEY SAY ABOUT LEE SOYOUN

Lee Soyoun's four poems including "The Origin of Prenatal Brain Education" riveted the judging panel immediately. The lyrical wording and delicately wrought sentences give the poems an allure while the variations in tone add lushness. Style notwithstanding, the poems proceed with neither overstatement nor understatement, arriving at their exact destinations in terms of thought process. All four poems display consistent quality, assuring us of their poetic achievement.

Poets Kwon Hyuk-ung, Kim Ki-taek, and Choi Seung-ho,
"Judges' Comments,"
Hankyung New Writer Award, 2014

The poet Lee Soyoun communicates through wounds as a way of both revealing herself to others and understanding those others. In her work, bleeding from a wound amounts to a poetic testimonial. . . . Hence, the poetry collection [*I Need a Girl Who Will Die Slowly*] does not present wounds as ruptures that destroy the ego. Wounds constitute inevitable fate insofar as life is embraced. In a way, the poet appears to verge on death, but by embracing wounds, she draws closer to life.

Literary Critic Park Dong-eok, "Ego as Skin,"
Munhakdongne, Fall 2020

K-POET
Nearly All Happiness

Written by Lee Soyoun
Translated by Sunnie Chae
Published by ASIA Publishers
Address 445, Hoedong-gil, Paju-si, Gyeonggi-do, Korea
Tel (8231).944.5058
Email bookasia@hanmail.net
Homepage Address www.bookasia.org

ISBN 979-11-5662-317-5 (set) | 979-11-5662-612-1 (04810)
First published in Korea by ASIA Publishers 2022

This book is published with the support of the Literature Translation Institute of Korea (LTI Korea).

K-픽션 한국 젊은 소설

최근에 발표된 단편소설 중 가장 우수하고 흥미로운 작품을 엄선하여 출간하는 〈K-픽션〉은 한국문학의 생생한 현장을 국내외 독자들과 실시간으로 공유하고자 기획되었습니다. 원작의 재미와 품격을 최대한 살린 〈K-픽션〉 시리즈는 매 계절마다 새로운 작품을 선보입니다.

001 버핏과의 저녁 식사-**박민규** Dinner with Buffett-**Park Min-gyu**
002 아르판-**박형서** Arpan-**Park hyoung su**
003 애드벌룬-**손보미** Hot Air Balloon-**Son Bo-mi**
004 나의 클린트 이스트우드-**오한기** My Clint Eastwood-**Oh Han-ki**
005 이베리아의 전갈-**최민우** Dishonored-**Choi Min-woo**
006 양의 미래-**황정은** Kong's Garden-**Hwang Jung-eun**
007 대니-**윤이형** Danny-**Yun I-hyeong**
008 퇴근-**천명관** Homecoming-**Cheon Myeong-kwan**
009 옥화-**금희** Ok-hwa-**Geum Hee**
010 시차-**백수린** Time Difference-**Baik Sou linne**
011 올드 맨 리버-**이장욱** Old Man River-**Lee Jang-wook**
012 권순찬과 착한 사람들-**이기호** Kwon Sun-chan and Nice People-**Lee Ki-ho**
013 알바생 자르기-**장강명** Fired-**Chang Kangmyoung**
014 어디로 가고 싶으신가요-**김애란** Where Would You Like To Go?-**Kim Ae-ran**
015 세상에서 가장 비싼 소설-**김민정** The World's Most Expensive Novel-**Kim Min-jung**
016 체스의 모든 것-**김금희** Everything About Chess-**Kim Keum-hee**
017 할로윈-**정한아** Halloween-**Chung Han-ah**
018 그 여름-**최은영** The Summer-**Choi Eunyoung**
019 어느 피씨주의자의 종생기-**구병모** The Story of P.C.-**Gu Byeong-mo**
020 모르는 영역-**권여선** An Unknown Realm-**Kwon Yeo-sun**
021 4월의 눈-**손원평** April Snow-**Sohn Won-pyung**
022 서우-**강화길** Seo-u-**Kang Hwa-gil**
023 가출-**조남주** Run Away-**Cho Nam-joo**
024 연애의 감정학-**백영옥** How to Break Up Like a Winner-**Baek Young-ok**
025 창모-**우다영** Chang-mo-**Woo Da-young**
026 검은 방-**정지아** The Black Room-**Jeong Ji-a**
027 도쿄의 마야-**장류진** Maya in Tokyo-**Jang Ryu-jin**
028 홀리데이 홈-**편혜영** Holiday Home-**Pyun Hye-young**
029 해피 투게더-**서장원** Happy Together-**Seo Jang-won**
030 골드러시-**서수진** Gold Rush-**Seo Su-jin**
031 당신이 보고 싶어하는 세상-**장강명** The World You Want to See-**Chang Kang-Myoung**

바이링궐 에디션 한국 대표 소설

한국문학의 가장 중요하고 첨예한 문제의식을 가진 작가들의 대표작을 주제별로 선정!
하버드 한국학 연구원 및 세계 각국의 한국문학 전문 번역진이 참여한 번역 시리즈!
미국 하버드대학교와 컬럼비아대학교 동아시아학과, 캐나다 브리티시컬럼비아대학교 아시아학과 등 해외 대학에서 교재로 채택!

바이링궐 에디션 한국 대표 소설 set 1

분단 Division

01 병신과 머저리-**이청준** The Wounded-**Yi Cheong-jun**
02 어둠의 혼-**김원일** Soul of Darkness-**Kim Won-il**
03 순이삼촌-**현기영** Sun-i Samch'on-**Hyun Ki-young**
04 엄마의 말뚝 1-**박완서** Mother's Stake I-**Park Wan-suh**
05 유형의 땅-**조정래** The Land of the Banished-**Jo Jung-rae**

산업화 Industrialization

06 무진기행-**김승옥** Record of a Journey to Mujin-**Kim Seung-ok**
07 삼포 가는 길-**황석영** The Road to Sampo-**Hwang Sok-yong**
08 아홉 켤레의 구두로 남은 사내-**윤흥길** The Man Who Was Left as Nine Pairs of Shoes-**Yun Heung-gil**
09 돌아온 우리의 친구-**신상웅** Our Friend's Homecoming-**Shin Sang-ung**
10 원미동 시인-**양귀자** The Poet of Wŏnmi-dong-**Yang Kwi-ja**

여성 Women

11 중국인 거리-**오정희** Chinatown-**Oh Jung-hee**
12 풍금이 있던 자리-**신경숙** The Place Where the Harmonium Was-**Shin Kyung-sook**
13 하나코는 없다-**최윤** The Last of Hanak'o-**Ch'oe Yun**
14 인간에 대한 예의-**공지영** Human Decency-**Gong Ji-young**
15 빈처-**은희경** Poor Man's Wife-**Eun Hee-kyung**

바이링궐 에디션 한국 대표 소설 set 2

자유 Liberty

16 필론의 돼지-**이문열** Pilon's Pig-**Yi Mun-yol**
17 슬로우 불릿-**이대환** Slow Bullet-**Lee Dae-hwan**
18 직선과 독가스-**임철우** Straight Lines and Poison Gas-**Lim Chul-woo**
19 깃발-**홍희담** The Flag-**Hong Hee-dam**
20 새벽 출정-**방현석** Off to Battle at Dawn-**Bang Hyeon-seok**

사랑과 연애 Love and Love Affairs

21 별을 사랑하는 마음으로-**윤후명** With the Love for the Stars-**Yun Hu-myong**
22 목련공원-**이승우** Magnolia Park-**Lee Seung-u**
23 칼에 찔린 자국-**김인숙** Stab-**Kim In-suk**
24 회복하는 인간-**한강** Convalescence-**Han Kang**
25 트렁크-**정이현** In the Trunk-**Jeong Yi-hyun**

남과 북 South and North

26 판문점-**이호철** Panmunjom-**Yi Ho-chol**
27 수난 이대-**하근찬** The Suffering of Two Generations-**Ha Geun-chan**
28 분지-**남정현** Land of Excrement-**Nam Jung-hyun**
29 봄 실상사-**정도상** Spring at Silsangsa Temple-**Jeong Do-sang**
30 은행나무 사랑-**김하기** Gingko Love-**Kim Ha-kee**

바이링궐 에디션 한국 대표 소설 set 3

서울 Seoul

31 눈사람 속의 검은 항아리-**김소진** The Dark Jar within the Snowman-**Kim So-jin**
32 오후, 가로지르다-**하성란** Traversing Afternoon-**Ha Seong-nan**
33 나는 봉천동에 산다-**조경란** I Live in Bongcheon-dong-**Jo Kyung-ran**
34 그렇습니까? 기린입니다-**박민규** Is That So? I'm A Giraffe-**Park Min-gyu**
35 성탄특선-**김애란** Christmas Specials-**Kim Ae-ran**

전통 Tradition

36 무자년의 가을 사흘-**서정인** Three Days of Autumn, 1948-**Su Jung-in**
37 유자소전-**이문구** A Brief Biography of Yuja-**Yi Mun-gu**
38 향기로운 우물 이야기-**박범신** The Fragrant Well-**Park Bum-shin**
39 월행-**송기원** A Journey under the Moonlight-**Song Ki-won**
40 협죽도 그늘 아래-**성석제** In the Shade of the Oleander-**Song Sok-ze**

아방가르드 Avant-garde

41 아겔다마-**박상륭** Akeldama-**Park Sang-ryoong**
42 내 영혼의 우물-**최인석** A Well in My Soul-**Choi In-seok**
43 당신에 대해서-**이인성** On You-**Yi In-seong**
44 회색 時-**배수아** Time In Gray-**Bae Su-ah**
45 브라운 부인-**정영문** Mrs. Brown-**Jung Young-moon**

바이링궐 에디션 한국 대표 소설 set 4

디아스포라 Diaspora

46 속옷-**김남일** Underwear-**Kim Nam-il**
47 상하이에 두고 온 사람들-**공선옥** People I Left in Shanghai-**Gong Sun-ok**
48 모두에게 복된 새해-**김연수** Happy New Year to Everyone-**Kim Yeon-su**
49 코끼리-**김재영** The Elephant-**Kim Jae-young**
50 먼지별-**이경** Dust Star-**Lee Kyung**

가족 Family

51 혜자의 눈꽃-**천승세** Hye-ja's Snow-Flowers-**Chun Seung-sei**
52 아베의 가족-**전상국** Ahbe's Family-**Jeon Sang-guk**
53 문 앞에서-**이동하** Outside the Door-**Lee Dong-ha**
54 그리고, 축제-**이혜경** And Then the Festival-**Lee Hye-kyung**
55 봄밤-**권여선** Spring Night-**Kwon Yeo-sun**

유머 Humor

56 오늘의 운세-**한창훈** Today's Fortune-**Han Chang-hoon**
57 새-**전성태** Bird-**Jeon Sung-tae**
58 밀수록 다시 가까워지는-**이기호** So Far, and Yet So Near-**Lee Ki-ho**
59 유리방패-**김중혁** The Glass Shield-**Kim Jung-hyuk**
60 전당포를 찾아서-**김종광** The Pawnshop Chase-**Kim Chong-kwang**

바이링궐 에디션 한국 대표 소설 set 5

관계 Relationship

61 도둑견습 – **김주영** Robbery Training-**Kim Joo-young**
62 사랑하라, 희망 없이 – **윤영수** Love, Hopelessly-**Yun Young-su**
63 봄날 오후, 과부 셋 – **정지아** Spring Afternoon, Three Widows-**Jeong Ji-a**
64 유턴 지점에 보물지도를 묻다 - **윤성희** Burying a Treasure Map at the U-turn-**Yoon Sung-hee**
65 쁘이거나 쯔이거나 - **백가흠** Puy, Thuy, Whatever-**Paik Ga-huim**

일상의 발견 Discovering Everyday Life

66 나는 음식이다 – **오수연** I Am Food-**Oh Soo-yeon**
67 트럭 – **강영숙** Truck-**Kang Young-sook**
68 통조림 공장 - **편혜영** The Canning Factory-**Pyun Hye-young**
69 꽃 – **부희령** Flowers-**Pu Hee-ryoung**
70 피의일요일 – **윤이형** BloodySunday-**Yun I-hyeong**

금기와 욕망 Taboo and Desire

71 북소리 - **송영** Drumbeat-**Song Yong**
72 발칸의 장미를 내게 주었네 - **정미경** He Gave Me Roses of the Balkans-**Jung Mi-kyung**
73 아무도 돌아오지 않는 밤 - **김숨** The Night Nobody Returns Home-**Kim Soom**
74 젓가락여자 - **천운영** Chopstick Woman-**Cheon Un-yeong**
75 아직 일어나지 않은 일 - **김미월** What Has Yet to Happen-**Kim Mi-wol**

바이링궐 에디션 한국 대표 소설 set 6

운명 Fate

76 언니를 놓치다 - **이경자** Losing a Sister-**Lee Kyung-ja**
77 아들 - **윤정모** Father and Son-**Yoon Jung-mo**
78 명두 - **구효서** Relics-**Ku Hyo-seo**
79 모독 - **조세희** Insult-**Cho Se-hui**
80 화요일의 강 - **손홍규** Tuesday River-**Son Hong-gyu**

미의 사제들 Aesthetic Priests

81 고수 - **이외수** Grand Master-**Lee Oisoo**
82 말을 찾아서 - **이순원** Looking for a Horse-**Lee Soon-won**
83 상춘곡 - **윤대녕** Song of Everlasting Spring-**Youn Dae-nyeong**
84 삭매와 자미 - **김별아** Sakmae and Jami-**Kim Byeol-ah**
85 저만치 혼자서 - **김훈** Alone Over There-**Kim Hoon**

식민지의 벌거벗은 자들 The Naked in the Colony

86 감자 - **김동인** Potatoes-**Kim Tong-in**
87 운수 좋은 날 - **현진건** A Lucky Day-**Hyŏn Chin'gŏn**
88 탈출기 - **최서해** Escape-**Ch'oe So-hae**
89 과도기 - **한설야** Transition-**Han Seol-ya**
90 지하촌 - **강경애** The Underground Village-**Kang Kyŏng-ae**

바이링궐 에디션 한국 대표 소설 set 7

백치가 된 식민지 지식인 Colonial Intellectuals Turned "Idiots"

91 날개 - **이상** Wings-**Yi Sang**
92 김 강사와 T 교수 - **유진오** Lecturer Kim and Professor T-**Chin-O Yu**
93 소설가 구보씨의 일일 - **박태원** A Day in the Life of Kubo the Novelist-**Pak Taewon**
94 비 오는 길 - **최명익** Walking in the Rain-**Ch'oe Myŏngik**
95 빛 속에 - **김사량** Into the Light-**Kim Sa-ryang**

한국의 잃어버린 얼굴 Traditional Korea's Lost Faces

96 봄·봄 – **김유정** Spring, Spring–**Kim Yu-jeong**
97 벙어리 삼룡이 – **나도향** Samnyong the Mute–**Na Tohyang**
98 달밤 – **이태준** An Idiot's Delight–**Yi T'ae-jun**
99 사랑손님과 어머니 – **주요섭** Mama and the Boarder–**Chu Yo-sup**
100 갯마을 – **오영수** Seaside Village–**Oh Yeongsu**

해방 전후(前後) Before and After Liberation

101 소망 – **채만식** Juvesenility–**Ch'ae Man-Sik**
102 두 파산 – **염상섭** Two Bankruptcies–**Yom Sang-Seop**
103 풀잎 – **이효석** Leaves of Grass–**Lee Hyo-seok**
104 맥 – **김남천** Barley–**Kim Namch'on**
105 꺼삐딴 리 – **전광용** Kapitan Ri–**Chŏn Kwangyong**

전후(戰後) Korea After the Korean War

106 소나기 – **황순원** The Cloudburst–**Hwang Sun-Won**
107 등신불 – **김동리** Tŭngsin-bul–**Kim Tong-ni**
108 요한 시집 – **장용학** The Poetry of John–**Chang Yong-hak**
109 비 오는 날 – **손창섭** Rainy Days–**Son Chang-sop**
110 오발탄 – **이범선** A Stray Bullet–**Lee Beomseon**